The
Kids Can Press
French & English
Word Book

Kids Can Press Ltd. acknowledges with
appreciation the assistance of the Canada
Council and the Ontario Arts Council in the
production of this book.

Canadian Cataloguing in Publication Data

The Kids Can Press French & English Word
Book

Text in English and French
ISBN 1-55074-022-9

1. Picture dictionaries, English—Juvenile
literature. 2. Picture dictionaries, French—
Juvenile literature. 3. English language—
Glossaries, vocabularies, etc.—Juvenile
literature. 4. French language—Glossaries,
vocabularies, etc.—Juvenile literature. I. Farris,
Katherine. II. Hendry, Linda.

PE1629.K5 1991   j423'.I   C90-095481-7E

Kids Can Press Ltd.
585½ Bloor Street West
Toronto, Ontario, Canada
M6G 1K5.

Book design by Michael Solomon
Printed and bound in Hong Kong

91 0 9 8 7 6 5 4 3

The Kids Can Press French & English Word Book

Edited by
Katherine Farris

Illustrated by
Linda Hendry

Kids Can Press Ltd.
Toronto

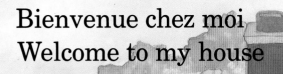

Bienvenue chez moi
Welcome to my house

des bardeaux
shingles

un toit
roof

une chambre
bedroom

une fenêtre
window

un porche
porch

un mur
wall

un salon
living room

un sous-sol
basement

un perron
front steps

une cheminée
chimney

une salle de bain
bathroom

un escalier
stairs

une jardinière
flower box

un garage
garage

une porte
door

une cuisine
kitchen

une corde à linge
clothes line

une salle à manger
dining room

un jardin
garden

un portillon
gate

une clôture
fence

Voici ma famille
Meet my family

un grand-père
grandfather

un cousin
cousin

un père
father

une cousine
cousin

un frère
brother

une mère
mother

un bébé
baby

un chien
dog

une soeur
sister

6

une grand-mère
grandmother

une tante
aunt

un oncle
uncle

une nièce
niece

un neveu
nephew

des jumelles
twins

un chat
cat

une arrière-grand-mère
great grandmother

un arrière-grand-père
great grandfather

C'est le matin
It's a new day

se brosser les dents
brush your teeth

prendre un bain
take a bath

dormir
sleep

lire
read

s'asseoir
sit

faire frire un oeuf
fry an egg

manger
eat

boire
drink

tondre la pelouse
mow the lawn

arroser les plantes
water the plants

se battre
fight

monter l'escalier
go up the stairs

prendre une douche
take a shower

se sécher les cheveux
dry your hair

repasser
iron

pleurer
cry

marcher
walk

tomber
fall

rire
laugh

regarder la télévision
watch tv

descendre l'escalier
go down the stairs

Bonjour!
Good morning!

un blouson
jacket

un chapeau
hat

une chemise
shirt

des bottes
boots

des souliers
shoes

des chaussettes
socks

un peignoir
bathrobe

une robe
dress

des lacets
shoelaces

une culotte
underpants

des chaussures de sport
running shoes

un maillot de corps
undershirt

un sweat-shirt
sweatshirt

un tee-shirt
T-shirt

une jupe
skirt

un short
shorts

un pantalon
pants

une chemise de nuit
nightgown

un pull-over
sweater

un gilet
vest

une tuque
hat

un pyjama
pyjamas

une mitaine
mitten

une écharpe
scarf

des pantoufles
slippers

un manteau
coat

une ceinture
belt

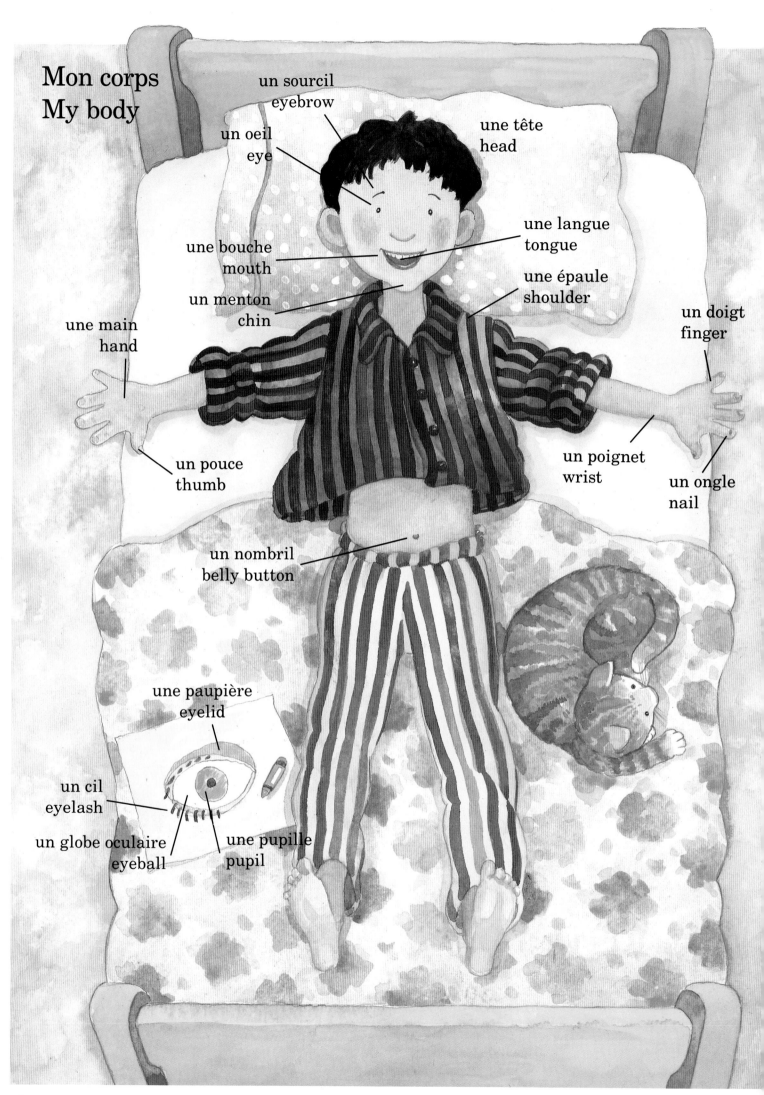

Mon corps
My body

un sourcil
eyebrow

un oeil
eye

une tête
head

une langue
tongue

une bouche
mouth

une épaule
shoulder

un menton
chin

une main
hand

un doigt
finger

un pouce
thumb

un poignet
wrist

un ongle
nail

un nombril
belly button

une paupière
eyelid

un cil
eyelash

un globe oculaire
eyeball

une pupille
pupil

12

des yeux
eyes

des cheveux
hair

des cheveux châtains
brunette

une joue
cheek

une oreille
ear

des cheveux blonds
blond

un nez
nose

une dent
tooth

des cheveux roux
red head

un cou
neck

un coude
elbow

un dos
back

un bras
arm

un genou
knee

une jambe
leg

un orteil
toe

un pied
foot

une cheville
ankle

On déjeune
Breakfast time

un couteau
knife

une assiette
plate

une fourchette
fork

une cuillère
spoon

du beurre
butter

des croissants
croissants

une tasse
cup

un oeuf
egg

du sucre
sugar

une rôtie
toast

une théière
teapot

un grille-pain
toaster

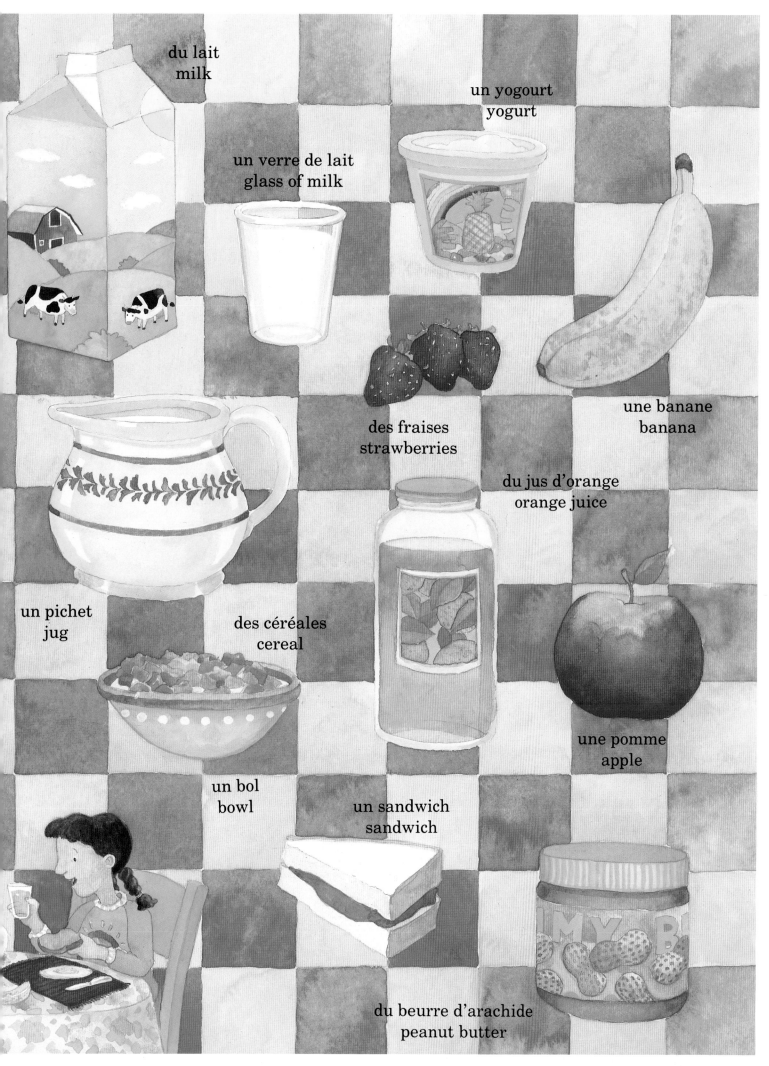

du lait
milk

un yogourt
yogurt

un verre de lait
glass of milk

une banane
banana

des fraises
strawberries

du jus d'orange
orange juice

un pichet
jug

des céréales
cereal

une pomme
apple

un bol
bowl

un sandwich
sandwich

du beurre d'arachide
peanut butter

À l'école
At my school

1 un
2 deux
3 trois
4 quatre
5 cinq
6 six
7 sep

Hello
Bonjour
Hola

Buon giorno
Guten Tag

שלום
γειά σο
喂
こんにち

un tableau noir
blackboard

un globe terrestre
globe

un microscope
microscope

des livres
books

une professeure
teacher

un garçon
boy

une fille
girl

un aquarium
aquarium

un poisson rouge
goldfish

un bâton
de base-ball
baseball bat

un pupitre
school desk

des élèves
students

une cage
cage

un hamster
hamster

un gant de base-ball
baseball mitt

un livre
book

16

les planètes
planets

une horloge
clock

hult   neuf   dix

Bom dia
Goeden Dag
Goddag
Szerbusz

un calendrier
calendar

un lapin
rabbit

une marionnette
puppet

une carte du monde
map of the world

un piano
piano

un bureau
desk

une guitare
guitar

le soleil
sun

une poubelle
garbage can

une trompette
trumpet

un sac d'écolier
school knapsack

une flûte à bec
flute

un tambour
drum

des patins à roulettes
roller skates

un jeu
game

un tambourin
tambourine

17

Dans la classe
In my classroom

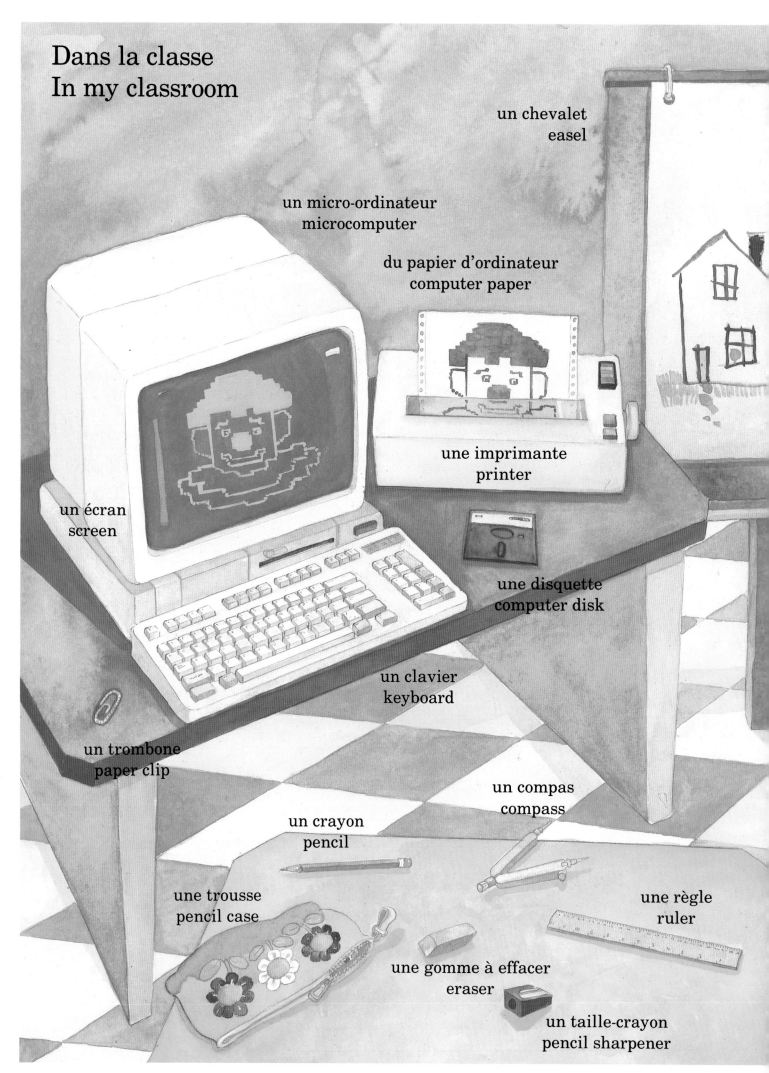

un chevalet
easel

un micro-ordinateur
microcomputer

du papier d'ordinateur
computer paper

une imprimante
printer

un écran
screen

une disquette
computer disk

un clavier
keyboard

un trombone
paper clip

un compas
compass

un crayon
pencil

une trousse
pencil case

une règle
ruler

une gomme à effacer
eraser

un taille-crayon
pencil sharpener

un dessin
picture

un crayon de couleur
pencil crayon

de la colle
glue

un pot de peinture
paint tin

des craies de cire
wax crayons

une boîte de couleurs
paint box

un pinceau
paintbrush

du ruban adhésif
sticky tape

des ciseaux
scissors

un dictionnaire
dictionary

une calculatrice
calculator

un stylo
pen

un livre de classe
textbook

un cahier
notebook

Ce que je fais à l'école
What I do at school

additionner
add

soustraire
subtract

donner à manger aux poissons
feed the fish

compter
count

étudier
study

se balancer
to swing

jouer
play

courir
run

sauter à la corde
skip with a rope

grimper
climb

écrire
write

peindre
paint

dessiner
draw

faire la sieste
nap

En excursion
Going on a trip

un gratte-ciel
skyscraper

des nuages
clouds

une ville
city

un village
village

une route
road

un autobus scolaire
schoolbus

un champ
field

une rivière
river

un zoo
zoo

un épouvantail
scarecrow

une étable
stable

un éléphant
elephant

un cygne
swan

une girafe
giraffe

22

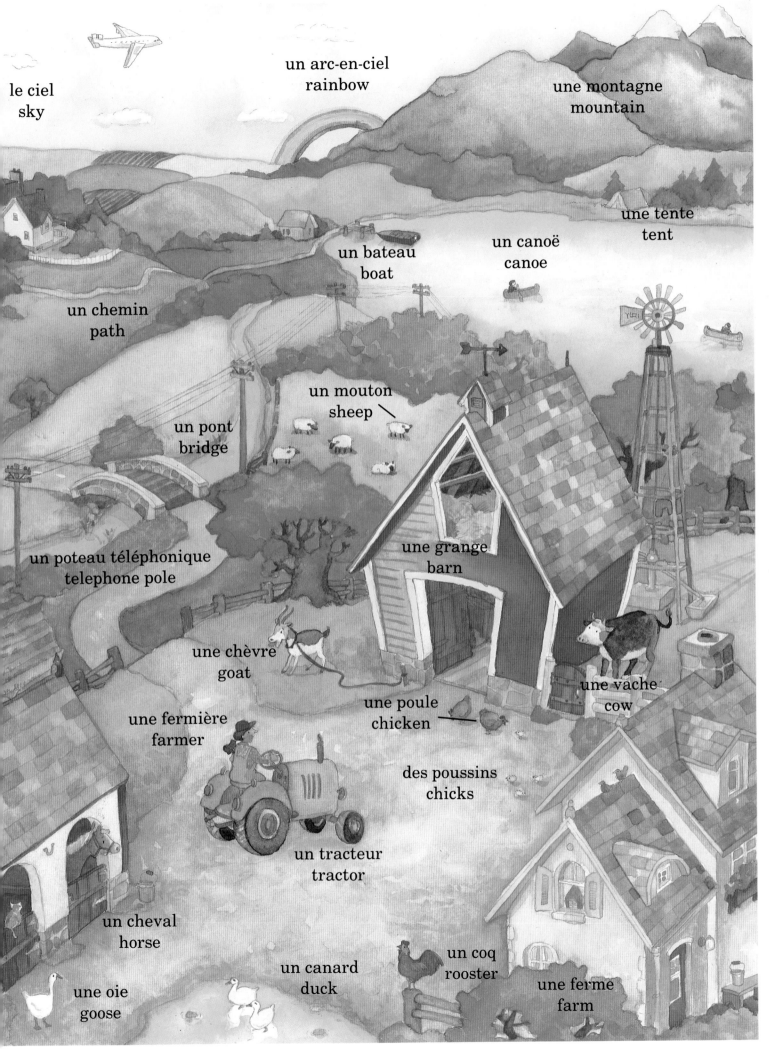

le ciel
sky

un arc-en-ciel
rainbow

une montagne
mountain

une tente
tent

un canoë
canoe

un bateau
boat

un chemin
path

un mouton
sheep

un pont
bridge

un poteau téléphonique
telephone pole

une grange
barn

une chèvre
goat

une vache
cow

une poule
chicken

une fermière
farmer

des poussins
chicks

un tracteur
tractor

un cheval
horse

un coq
rooster

un canard
duck

une ferme
farm

une oie
goose

23

Au zoo
A day at
the zoo

un évent
blowhole

une nageoire
flipper

un dauphin
dolphin

une carapace
shell

une tortue
tortoise

un groin
snout

un sanglier
boar

un bec
beak

un oiseau
bird

une aile
wing

la peau
hide

une plume
feather

une trompe d'éléphant
elephant's trunk

une défense d'éléphant
elephant's tusk

des bois
antlers

une queue
tail

un cerf
deer

un mouflon
mountain sheep

une corne
horn

un sabot
hoof

des moustaches
whiskers

un croc
fang

une crinière
mane

une lionne
lioness

le pelage
fur

un ours polaire
polar bear

une patte
paw

une griffe
claw

Mes animaux préférés au zoo
My favourite zoo animals

un chameau
camel

un flamant rose
pink flamingo

un phoque
seal

un hippopotame
hippopotamus

un buffle
buffalo

un kangourou
kangaroo

un pingouin
penguin

un gorille
gorilla

un serpent
snake

un singe
monkey

un toucan
toucan

un ours brun
brown bear

un crocodile
crocodile

un lion
lion

une souris
mouse

un perroquet
parrot

un tigre
tiger

une baleine
whale

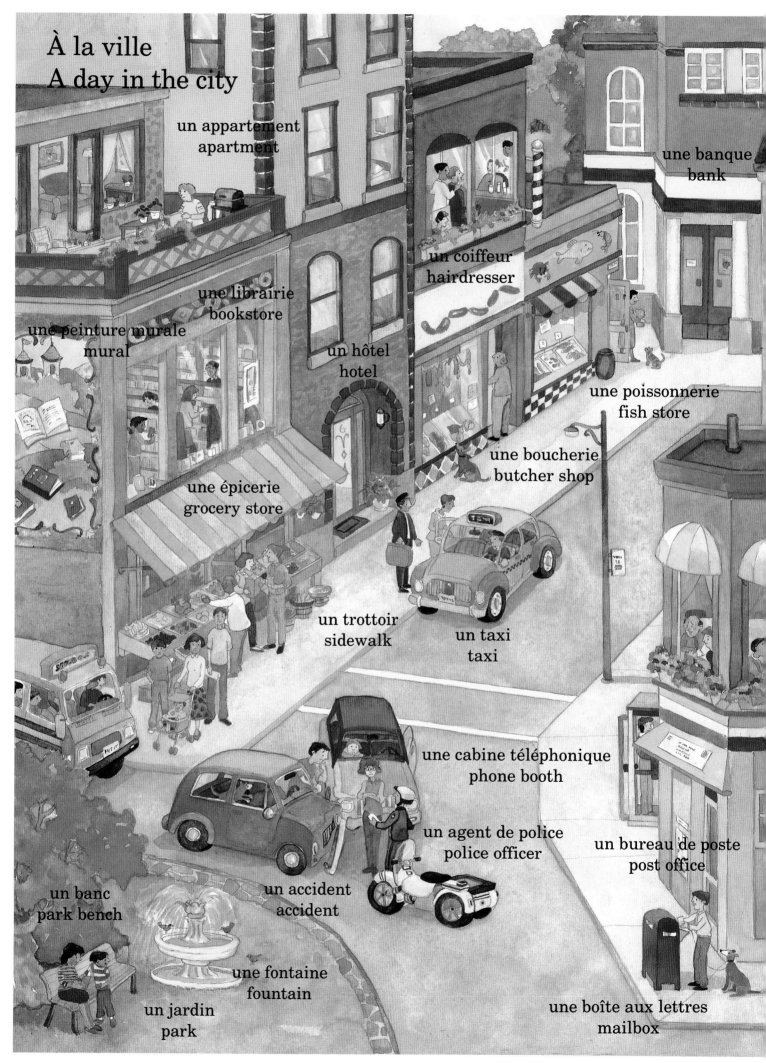

À la ville
A day in the city

un appartement
apartment

une banque
bank

un coiffeur
hairdresser

une librairie
bookstore

une peinture murale
mural

un hôtel
hotel

une poissonnerie
fish store

une boucherie
butcher shop

une épicerie
grocery store

un trottoir
sidewalk

un taxi
taxi

une cabine téléphonique
phone booth

un agent de police
police officer

un bureau de poste
post office

un banc
park bench

un accident
accident

une fontaine
fountain

un jardin
park

une boîte aux lettres
mailbox

28

un hôpital
hospital

un grand magasin
department store

un drapeau
flag

un mât
flagpole

une cycliste
cyclist

une caserne de pompiers
firehall

un restaurant
restaurant

une bouche d'incendie
fire hydrant

un cinéma
movie house

un marchand de fleurs
flower vendor

une piétonne
pedestrian

un kiosque à journaux
newsstand

une boulangerie
bakery

un passage pour piétons
pedestrian crossing

une plaque de rue
street sign

Au magasin
Going to the store

une caissière
cashier

un céleri
celery

une cliente
customer

une banane
banana

une caisse
cash register

un sac en papier
paper bag

un citron
lemon

un ananas
pineapple

une pêche
peach

une pomme
apple

une orange
orange

un pamplemousse
grapefruit

une poire
pear

un abricot
apricot

une framboise
raspberry

une prune
plum

une mangue
mango

une cerise
cherry

un melon d'eau
watermelon

des raisins
grapes

un avocat
avocado

des pois
peas

une laitue
lettuce

un concombre
cucumber

un épicier
grocer

une tomate
tomato

une carotte
carrot

un oignon
onion

une pomme de terre
potato

du maïs
corn

des haricots verts
green beans

Les moyens de transport
On the move

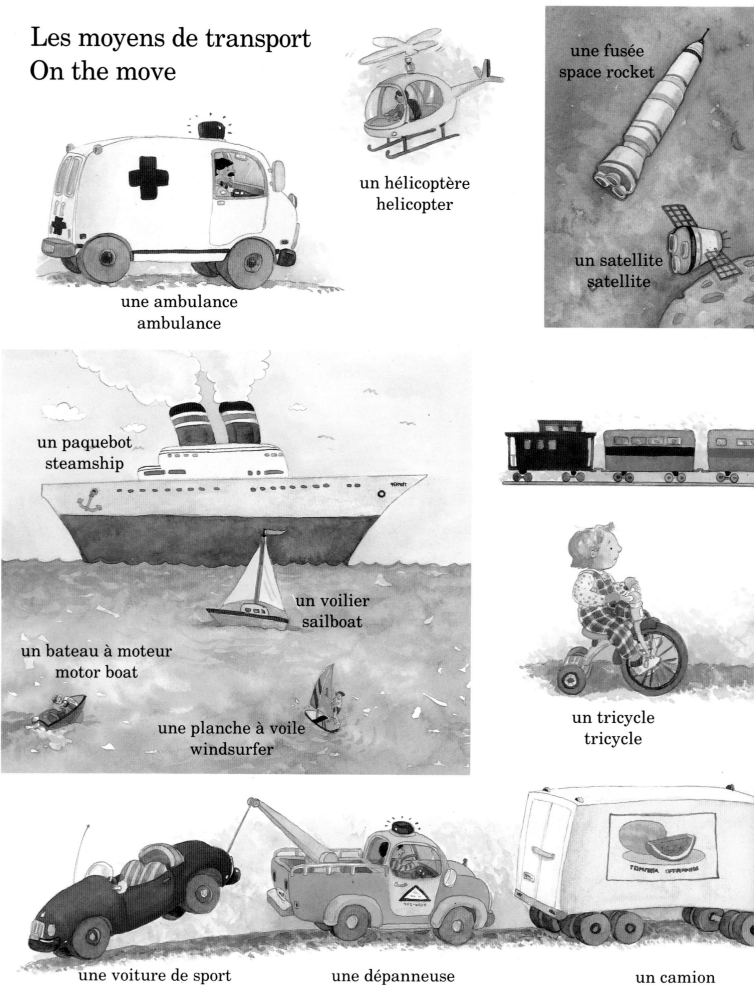

un hélicoptère
helicopter

une fusée
space rocket

un satellite
satellite

une ambulance
ambulance

un paquebot
steamship

un voilier
sailboat

un bateau à moteur
motor boat

une planche à voile
windsurfer

un tricycle
tricycle

une voiture de sport
sportscar

une dépanneuse
tow truck

un camion
truck

un jet
jet

un avion
plane

un autobus
bus

un train
train

une carte routière
roadmap

une clé
key

une roue
wheel

un pneu
tire

une bicyclette
bicycle

un chariot
wagon

un camion de livraison
delivery truck

une remorque
trailer

une roulotte
motor home

33

Dans mon jardin
In my backyard

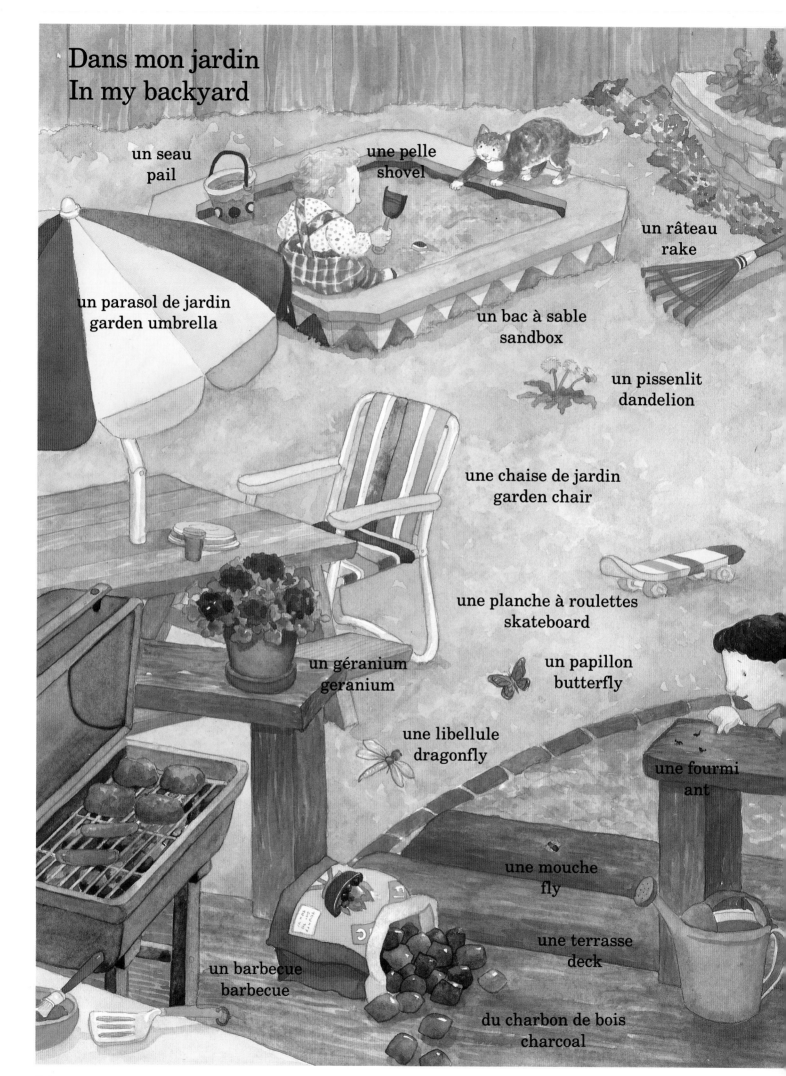

un seau
pail

une pelle
shovel

un râteau
rake

un parasol de jardin
garden umbrella

un bac à sable
sandbox

un pissenlit
dandelion

une chaise de jardin
garden chair

une planche à roulettes
skateboard

un géranium
geranium

un papillon
butterfly

une libellule
dragonfly

une fourmi
ant

une mouche
fly

une terrasse
deck

un barbecue
barbecue

du charbon de bois
charcoal

une hirondelle
swallow

une feuille
leaf

une tondeuse à gazon
lawnmower

un arbre
tree

une balançoire
swing

l'herbe
grass

un écureuil
squirrel

une pensée
pansy

une abeille
bee

un champignon
mushroom

une violette
violet

un tournesol
sunflower

un rouge-gorge
robin

une rose
rose

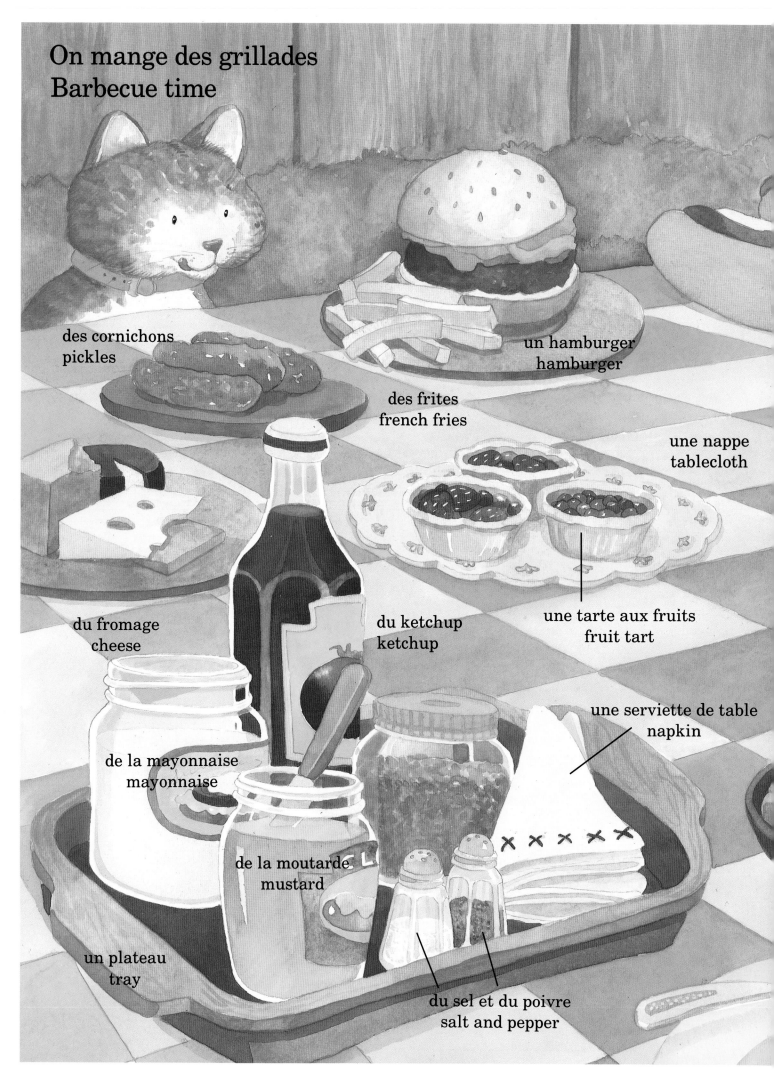

On mange des grillades
Barbecue time

des cornichons
pickles

un hamburger
hamburger

des frites
french fries

une nappe
tablecloth

du fromage
cheese

du ketchup
ketchup

une tarte aux fruits
fruit tart

de la mayonnaise
mayonnaise

une serviette de table
napkin

de la moutarde
mustard

un plateau
tray

du sel et du poivre
salt and pepper

des hot-dogs
hot dogs

de la glace
ice cream

du gâteau
cake

une corbeille de fruits
basket of fruit

une salade
salad

une boisson gazeuse
pop

une table
table

des biscuits
cookies

une salade de fruits
fruit salad

un jus de fruit
fruit juice

Mes couleurs préférées
My favourite colours

rose
pink

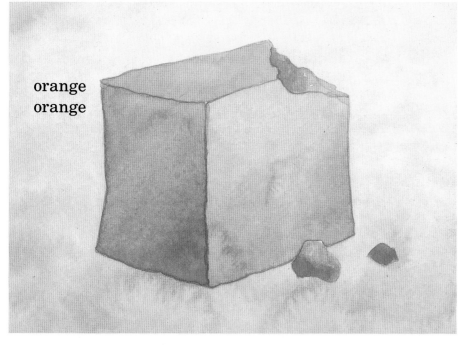

orange
orange

rouge
red

brun
brown

noir
black

vert
green

beige
beige

jaune
yellow

bleu
blue

gris
gray

violet
purple

blanc
white

De ma fenêtre
From my window

une étoile
star

une maison
house

une piscine
pool

un raton laveur
raccoon

une échelle
ladder

une poussette
stroller

une cabane dans un arbre
treehouse

un trottoir
sidewalk

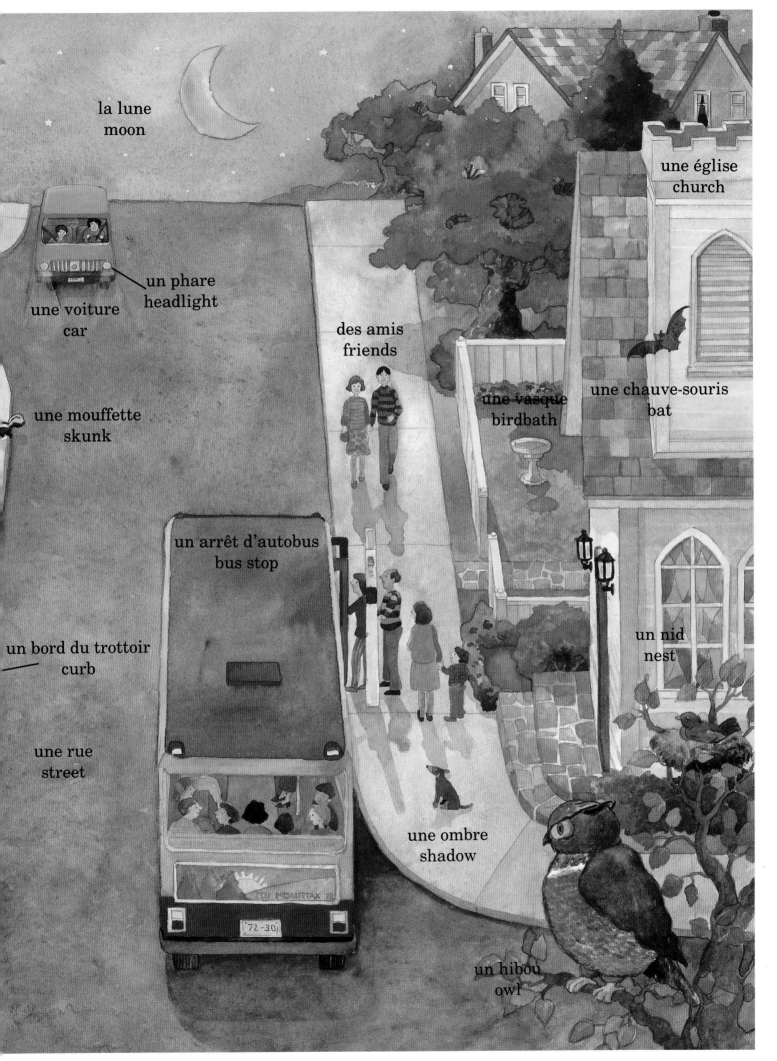

la lune
moon

une église
church

un phare
headlight

une voiture
car

des amis
friends

une vasque
birdbath

une chauve-souris
bat

une mouffette
skunk

un arrêt d'autobus
bus stop

un bord du trottoir
curb

un nid
nest

une rue
street

une ombre
shadow

un hibou
owl

41

Bonne nuit!
Good night!

un store
blind

un vase de fleurs
flower vase

un dessin
picture

des parents
parents

une lampe
lamp

un lit
bed

un drap
sheet

un réveille-matin
alarm clock

une couverture
blanket

un tiroir
drawer

des oreillers
pillows

une commode
chest of drawers

un tapis
carpet

une brosse à cheveux
hair brush

une chaise
chair

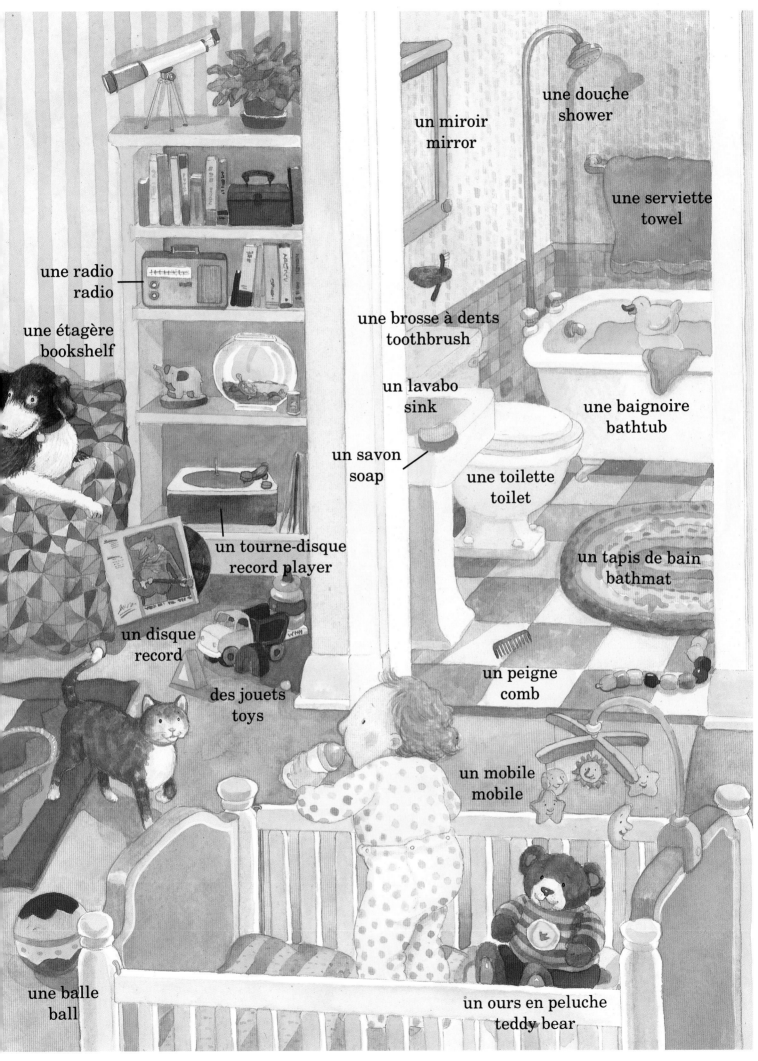

une radio
radio

une étagère
bookshelf

un miroir
mirror

une douche
shower

une serviette
towel

une brosse à dents
toothbrush

un lavabo
sink

une baignoire
bathtub

un savon
soap

une toilette
toilet

un tourne-disque
record player

un tapis de bain
bathmat

un disque
record

un peigne
comb

des jouets
toys

un mobile
mobile

une balle
ball

un ours en peluche
teddy bear

Quel est le contraire?
What's the opposite?

carré
square

rond
round

haut
high

bas
low

sur
on

sous
under

froid
cold

chaud
hot

plein
full

vide
empty

mou
soft

dur
hard

sec
dry

mouillé
wet

propre
clean

sale
dirty

ouvert
open

fermé
closed

grand
big

petit
small

heureux
happy

triste
sad

Word list

This is an alphabetical list of all the words in the book with their page numbers.

accident	28	brother	6	cucumber	31	flipper	24
add	20	brown	38	cup	14	flower box	5
alarm clock	42	brown bear	27	curb	41	flower vase	42
ambulance	32	brunette	13	customer	30	flower vendor	29
ankle	12	brush your teeth	8	cyclist	29	flute	17
ant	34	buffalo	26			fly	34
antlers	25	bus	33	dandelion	34	foot	13
apartment	28	bus stop	41	deck	35	fork	14
apple	30	butcher shop	28	deer	25	fountain	28
apricot	30	butter	14	delivery truck	33	french fries	36
aquarium	16	butterfly	34	department store	29	friends	41
arm	13			desk	17	front steps	4
aunt	7	cage	16	dictionary	19	fruit juice	37
avocado	31	cake	37	dining room	5	fruit salad	37
		calculator	19	dirty	45	fruit tart	36
baby	6	calendar	17	dog	6	fry an egg	8
back	13	camel	26	dolphin	24	full	44
bakery	29	canoe	23	door	5	fur	25
ball	43	car	41	dragonfly	34		
banana	15	carpet	42	draw	21	game	17
bank	28	carrot	31	drawer	42	garbage can	17
barbecue	34	cash register	30	dress	10	garden chair	34
barn	23	cashier	30	drink	8	garden umbrella	34
baseball bat	16	cat	7	drum	17	gate	5
baseball mitt	16	celery	30	dry	45	geranium	34
basement	4	cereal	15	dry your hair	9	giraffe	22
basket of fruit	37	chair	42	duck	23	girl	16
bat	41	charcoal	34			glass of milk	15
bathmat	43	cheek	12	ear	12	globe	16
bathrobe	10	cheese	36	easel	18	glue	19
bathroom	5	cherry	30	eat	8	go down the stairs	9
bathtub	43	chest of drawers	42	egg	14	go up the stairs	8
beak	24	chicken	23	elbow	13	goat	23
bed	42	chicks	23	elephant	22	goldfish	16
bedroom	4	chimney	5	elephant's trunk	24	goose	23
bee	35	chin	12	elephant's tusk	24	gorilla	26
beige	39	church	41	empty	44	grandfather	6
belly button	12	city	22	eraser	18	grandmother	7
belt	11	claw	25	eye	12	grapefruit	30
bicycle	33	clean	45	eyeball	12	grapes	31
big	45	climb	21	eyebrow	12	grass	35
bird	24	clock	17	eyelash	12	gray	39
birdbath	41	closed	45	eyelid	12	great grandfather	7
black	38	clothesline	5	eyes	13	great grandmother	7
blackboard	16	clouds	22			green	38
blanket	42	coat	11	fall	9	green beans	31
blind	42	cold	44	fang	25	grocer	31
blond	13	comb	43	farmer	23	grocery store	28
blowhole	24	compass	18	father	6	guitar	17
blue	39	computer disk	18	feather	24		
boar	24	computer paper	18	feed the fish	20	hair	13
boat	23	cookies	37	fence	5	hair brush	42
book	16	corn	31	field	22	hairdresser	28
books	16	count	20	fight	8	hamburger	36
bookshelf	43	cousin	6	fin	24	hamster	16
bookstore	28	cow	23	finger	12	hand	12
boots	10	crayons	19	fire hydrant	29	happy	45
bowl	15	crocodile	27	firehall	29	hard	45
boy	16	croissants	14	fish store	28	hat	10
bridge	23	cry	9	flag	29	head	12
				flagpole	29		

headlight	41	nail	12	potato	12	skunk	41
helicopter	32	nap	21	printer	18	sky	23
hide	24	napkin	36	pupil	12	skyscraper	22
high	44	neck	13	puppet	17	sleep	8
hippopotamus	26	nephew	7	purple	39	slippers	11
hoof	25	nest	41	pyjamas	11	small	45
horn	25	newsstand	29			snake	27
horse	23	niece	7	rabbit	17	snout	24
hospital	29	nightgown	11	raccoon	40	soap	43
hot	44	nose	13	radio	43	socks	10
hot dogs	37	notebook	19	rainbow	23	soft	45
hotel	28			rake	34	space rocket	32
house	40	on	44	raspberry	30	spoon	14
		onion	31	read	8	sportscar	32
ice cream	37	open	45	record	43	square	44
iron	9	orange	30	record player	43	squirrel	35
		orange juice	15	red	38	stable	22
jacket	10	owl	41	red head	13	stairs	5
jug	15			restaurant	29	star	40
		pail	34	river	22	steamship	32
kangaroo	26	paint	21	road	22	sticky tape	19
ketchup	36	paint box	19	roadmap	33	strawberries	15
key	33	paint tin	19	robin	35	street	41
keyboard	18	paintbrush	19	roller skates	17	street sign	29
kitchen	5	pansy	35	roof	4	stroller	40
knee	13	pants	11	rooster	23	students	16
knife	14	paper bag		rose	35	study	20
		paper clip	18	round	44	subtract	20
ladder	40	parents	42	ruler	18	sugar	14
lamp	42	park	28	run	21	sun	17
laugh	9	park bench	28	running shoes	10	sunflower	35
lawnmower	35	parrot	27			swallow	35
leaf	35	path	23	sad	45	swan	22
leg	13	paw	25	sailboat	32	sweater	11
lemon	30	peach	30	salad	37	sweatshirt	10
lettuce	31	peanut butter	15	salt	36	swing	35
lion	27	pear	30	sandbox	34		
lioness	25	peas	31	sandwich	15	T-shirt	10
living room	4	pedestrian	29	satellite	32	table	36
low	44	pedestrian crossing	29	scarecrow	22	tablecloth	36
		pen	19	scarf	11	tail	25
mailbox	28	pencil	18	school desk	16	take a bath	8
mane	25	pencil case	18	school knapsack	17	take a shower	9
mango	30	pencil crayon	19			tambourine	17
map of the world	17	pencil sharpener	18	scissors	19	taxi	28
mayonnaise	36	penguin	26	screen	18	teacher	16
microcomputer	18	pepper	36	seal	26	teapot	14
microscope	16	phone booth	28	shadow	41	teddy bear	43
milk	15	piano	17	sheep	23	telephone pole	23
mirror	43	pickles	36	sheet	42	tent	23
mitten	11	picture	42	shell	42	textbook	19
mobile	43	pillows	42	shingles	30	thumb	12
monkey	27	pineapple	30	shirt	38	tiger	27
moon	41	pink	38	shoelaces	10	tire	33
mother	6	pink flamingo	26	shoes	10	toast	14
motor boat	32	plane	33	shorts	33	toaster	14
motor home	33	planets	17	shoulder	17	toe	13
mountain	23	plate	14	shovel	34	toilet	43
mountain sheep	25	play	20	shower	43	tomato	31
mouse	27	plum	30	sidewalk	28	tongue	12
mouth	12	polar bear	25	sink	43	tooth	13
movie house	29	police officer	28	sister	6	toothbrush	43
mow the lawn	8	pool	40	sit	8	tortoise	24
mural	28	pop	37	skateboard	34	toucan	27
mushroom	35	porch	28	skip with a rope	21	tow truck	32
mustard	36	post office	28	skirt	11	towel	43